Big Machines At Work

Dump Trucks

By Jean Eick

SCHOLASTIC INC.

New York   Toronto   London   Auckland   Sydney
Mexico City   New Delhi   Hong Kong   Buenos Aires

For information regarding permission, write to:
The Child's World®, Inc.
P.O. Box 326
Chanhassen, Minnesota 55317

Photos: © 1998 David M. Budd Photography

ISBN 0-439-65057-7

Printed in the U.S.A.
First Scholastic printing, February 2004

Contents

On the Job

On the job, dump trucks work at **construction sites.** They carry heavy loads of dirt for the workers.

The big box on the back of this dump truck is being filled by a front-end loader.

Sometimes the dump truck bounces

as the huge load crashes into the box!

When the box is full, the dump truck takes the load to the place where it is to be dumped.

Beep, beep! The truck backs up

and then stops.

Up, up, up goes the heavy box. Long
metal arms called **hoists** push the
box up.

The dirt falls to the ground in

a big heap.

Bang! The box drops back down.

Off goes the dump truck to pick

up another load.

Climb Aboard!

Would you like to see where the driver sits? The dump truck's driver is called the **operator.** The operator uses a stick called a **lever** to make the hoists lift up the box.

The big mirrors on the side help the operator see behind him to back up.

Up Close

1. The cab

2. The hoists

3. The box

4. The lever

Glossary

construction sites (kun-STRUCK-shun SITES)
Construction sites are places where something is being built.
Dump trucks bring loads of dirt and other materials to and
from construction sites.

hoists (HOYSTS)
Hoists are the metal arms that lift the box of the dump truck.
They hold the box up until the dirt falls out.

lever (LEV-er)
A dump truck's lever is a stick with a round knob on the end. It
is used to raise the hoists.

operator (OPP-er-ay-ter)
The operator is the person who drives the dump truck and uses
the lever to make the hoists work.